One Day in the
PRAIRIE

To the Hainesport School students
Hello,

Jean Craighead George

7 · 8 · 96

Trophy Chapter Books by
Jean Craighead George:

One Day in the PRAIRIE

by Jean Craighead George

illustrated by Bob Marstall

HarperTrophy

A Division of HarperCollins*Publishers*

Library of Congress Cataloging-in-Publication Data
George, Jean Craighead, date
  One day in the prairie.
  Summary: The animals on a prairie wildlife refuge sense an
approaching tornado and seek protection before it touches down
and destroys everything in its path.
  ISBN 0-690-04564-6. — ISBN 0-690-04566-2 (lib. bdg.)
ISBN 0-06-442039-6 (pbk.)
  1. Prairie ecology—Juvenile literature. 2. Tornadoes—Juve-
nile literature. [1 . Prairie animals. 2. Prairies. 3. Tornadoes.]
I. Marstall, Bob, ill.   II. Title.
QH541.5P7G46   1986   85-48254
591.5′2643′097664   CIP
                                                         AC

❖
First Harper Trophy edition, 1996.

To Ellan Young, who braved the stampeding buffalo on the prairie with me.

One Day in the
PRAIRIE

Chapter 1

The sunrise lights up endless miles of yellowing grass on September 28. It is 6:55 A.M. in the prairie under a cloudless sky.

On a grassy mound in southwestern Oklahoma, a herd of buffalo moves restlessly. Despite the clear dawn, the air buzzes with electricity. It lifts the fur on the backs of the buffalo and tingles through their feet. They feel afraid. The mammoth

beasts sense a distant storm, as did their ancestors who survived storms and blizzards on the prairie for ten thousand years. The electricity hums to the west.

And yet the prairie grass is motionless where the buffalo stand. The killdeer walks quietly with its family. The prairie horned larks preen their feathers under clumps of grass. The gorgeous scissor-tailed flycatcher, with his long streaming tail, snatches a droning beetle. Only the trees in the river bottomlands seem to

speak of the danger the buffalo sense. They hold up their limbs as if before a gunman. Their leaves fall slowly and too soon.

At 7:15 A.M., twenty minutes after sunrise, the buffalo send out an odor of fear that can drive them to panic, and in panic to stampede.

They lower their heads to butt the unseen enemy.

At 7:30 A.M. they paw the ground. They are begging, but not for attention, which their pawing usually means.

3

They are begging out of nervousness, reacting to the electrically charged atoms. A tornado is forming.

The boss bull tramples the grass. The whites of his eyes flash as he picks an escape route through the flats of prairie dog town.

Henry Rush jumps out of his father's pickup truck at 7:40 A.M. and walks to a black oak tree in the middle of prairie dog town. He puts down his camera and pack, then glances back at his father.

"Pick me up at five fifteen," he calls. "I'll wait for you by the sign." He points to a board on a post that reads PRAIRIE WILDLIFE REFUGE. His father nods and waves.

A prairie dog pokes his head out of a cone-shaped burrow. Henry Rush laughs at his snappy eyes and pug nose and names him Red Dog. The little animal sees in all directions at once, because his eyes, which are high on his head and somewhat to the rear, give him global vision. He needs it. He is prey for almost all the predators of the prairie.

He sees the prairie sunflowers all around him, the earth at his feet, and the sky above him. He sees the golden eagle hunting her breakfast of prairie dog. Red Dog whistles a warning to the residents of prairie dog town, leaps up in the air, bends backward almost touching his head to his tail, drops on all fours, and dives into his burrow.

The eagle strikes near the creek and flies slowly off with a jackrabbit.

5

Moments pass. A meadowlark alights in prairie dog town and sings. Curlew parents call to reassemble their family, who hid from the eagle. Frogs pipe, toads croak, and the great blue heron resumes stalking fish in the shallows of Quanah Lake. All the creatures are saying, "The eagle is gone: All is well."

The buffalo do not hear the peaceful message. They are sensing the storm forming far beyond the curve of the horizon.

Chapter 2

Red Dog pops out of his burrow again. He is about sixteen inches long from his head to the tip of his tail. His small ears grow close to his head and do not get bruised when he runs through his narrow, tight tunnels. He is fat and pear-shaped. With a quick movement he crosses his front paws on his chest and calls to one of his two hundred towns- men.

Once there were billions of prairie dogs on the great plains of North America. After a century of people shooting, poisoning, and plowing their homes under, only a few hundred are alive today to brighten the grasslands with their charm and industry.

Their homeland, the prairie, is a biotic community, one where all living things depend either directly or indirectly on the sun-made grass. There are those who eat the grass (buffalo, prairie dogs, jackrabbits, deer, elk, antelope, many birds and insects) and there are those who eat the grass eaters (wolves, eagles, prairie falcons, coyotes, bobcats, owls, skunks, badgers, shrikes, and people).

The grasses are the prairie's great resource. More than two hundred different kinds festoon North America's meadow. Their wonderful names were thought up by Indian and prairie poets: goose grass, arrowfeather threeawn, big bluestem, Indian grass, weeping love grass, beaded spanglegrass, tumble grass, puffsheath dropseed, and the devil's darning needle, to name a few.

The prairie is a living community, like a forest, except that grass takes the place of trees. It covers one third of the United States and much of southern Canada. Stretched between the Appalachian

9

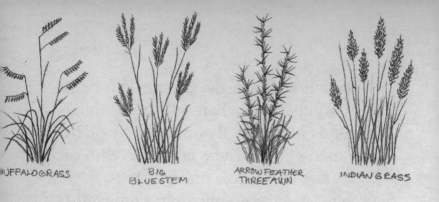

BUFFALOGRASS   BIG BLUESTEM   ARROW FEATHER THREE AWN   INDIAN GRASS

Mountains and the Rocky Mountains, America's fertile meadowland covers two million square miles. Other prairies that grow on the earth are the pampas of Argentina, the llanos in northern South America, the steppes of Eurasia, and the high velds of South Africa.

The American prairie shapes itself into three parts: the tall-grass prairie in the east, the medium-grass prairie in the midlands, and the short-grass prairie on the dry western edge. The great meadow is not entirely smooth and flat. Small, ancient mountains sit upon it, and it rolls in great land waves carved by the many rivers that wind through it. It is pocked with thousands and thousands of gleaming lakes and swamps that were gouged by the ice of the glaciers.

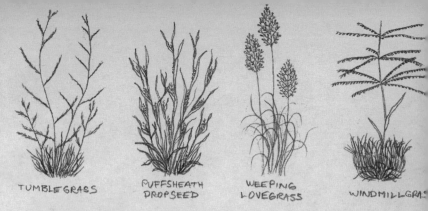

TUMBLEGRASS   PUFFSHEATH   WEEPING   WINDMILLGRASS
               DROPSEED   LOVEGRASS

The Prairie Wildlife Refuge, where the buffalo herd mills and Henry Rush focuses his camera, is a wild prairie. All the communities are represented here— the tall-, medium-, and short-grass communities; the river bottomlands with their many trees; the lakes with their reeds and sedges; and the mountain forests.

This beautiful parcel of prairieland once belonged to the Wichita Indians. Their gods, they believed, dwelled on Sacred Mountain, guarding the land. They seem to have guarded it well, for this speck of wilderness has been spared cultivation. The wheat and corn grains that make the rest of the prairie the world's most productive farmland were never planted here. The Wichitas'

11

land is much as it was before Europeans came to America.

The herd of wild buffalo that grazes the prairie grasses is a remnant of the sixty million animals that once lived on the original prairie. Another ghost from the past is a herd of longhorn steer, a mix of Spanish black cattle and the durable Mexican common cattle. They can withstand heat, drought, deluge, tornado, and blizzard. They can climb mountains like goats. The longhorns were turned loose after the Texas Revolution of 1836, then survived and grew in number until there were more than ten million on the prairie at the time of the Civil War. But the armies needed food. Cowboys rounded them up and drove them to the railroad heads in Oklahoma and Kansas. By 1900 the longhorns were almost extinct. Only a few remained on private estates and ranches.

Twenty years passed before a bull and several cows were brought to the wildlife refuge and set free to multiply.

Other wild things from the past still flourishing on this speck of original prairie are 208 wild grasses, the prairie dog town, more than a hundred varieties of wildflowers, 230 different kinds of birds, 32 types of salamanders, toads, and frogs, and 24 species of snakes.

Chapter 3

At 8:30 A.M. Henry Rush has the film in his camera and is lying on his belly, waiting for action in prairie dog town. A national magazine wants a photograph of a prairie dog doing a back flip, and Henry Rush is determined to get one. A back flip is to a prairie dog what someone yelling "fire" is to us. But the

flip is body language, a silent shriek of danger to attract the attention of animals who live close to the ground. One good back flip sends all the prairie dogs who see it into their burrows and underground tunnels.

Dark clouds appear on the flat western horizon. The temperature rises on the Oklahoma prairie. Autumn flowers reach up to the light. Hot and cold air mix in the distance and spiral into black thunderheads.

The buffalo smell the ozone from the mix. Their hoofs click. Dust rises. The boss bull stops eating. He rechecks his herd's escape route through prairie dog town. He does not see Henry Rush in the path, for Henry is lying as still as a stone, as inconspicuous to the bull as a grain of sand on the enormous prairie.

At 11 A.M. a breeze from the west stirs the damp hair on Henry Rush's temple. He does not give it a thought, for the prairie dog town is busy. Fifty or sixty of the townsmen are popping in and out of

their burrows. Some watch for enemies, others scurry to the meadow at the edge of their three-acre town, gathering seeds of the grasses and wildflowers. They stuff them into their cheeks and carry them to their underground pantries. A few dig, shooting dirt high into the air as they mend or improve their miles of tunnels.

The sentinels sit on twelve-inch-high cones of dirt, their front paws folded on their chests. They look like small tree stumps as they scan the grass, the sky, the earth, watching for eagles and

coyotes and hawks and weasels and minks and people.

No matter what the job—gatherer, housekeeper, or sentinel—all the prairie dogs bark to each other as they run about; hence their name prairie *dog* rather than prairie marmot or squirrel, which would be more correct. They are not dogs.

Red Dog whistles with the shrillness of a policeman's whistle, jumps into the air, and bends backward so far his head nearly touches his rump. Then he falls to the earth.

"Missed it," snorts Henry Rush.
"Missed the quintessential picture of the
back flip." He snaps his fingers, then
looks for the source of the danger. There
is much for a prairie dog to be worried
about. A coyote is moving through the
tall grass beside Quanah Creek. An elk,
whose huge platter-sized hoofs can
smash a prairie dog cone to dust, is
standing under a pecan tree not far away.

The breeding season of the elk began
this September day, and he has not eaten
all morning. He will not eat until
December, when the breeding season is
over and his harem is won and bred.
The magnificent bull elk bellows. Henry

Rush sees him toss his huge antlers, sees his thick neck and golden rump, and sees him suddenly startle. A wind from the west has alarmed him. He should not be afraid of the wind, Henry reasons. Elk like the wind. He has seen them stand quietly with their heads turned into it as if enjoying its motion.

"Interesting," he muses. "I always learn something new out here."

Chapter 4

The buffalo stop milling and face their escape route. The calves are in the middle of the herd, their mothers close by. The bulls are on the outside of the ring. The whites of their eyes flash.

The boss bull nudges a yellow-orange calf who was born only three days ago. The little animal trots close to him. For the first few days of a calf's life, the father buffalo takes charge of it. He bunts it to cross creeks, pushes it up hills, shoves it into the center of the herd when the coyote stalks and the winds tell tales of coming danger. The bull nudges the little orange calf into the center of the ring.

The breeding season of the buffalo is almost over. It began in June, when the ground plums, the pasqueflowers, and the buttercups were blooming in huge swatches. It is ending with the blooming of October's purple Townsendia.

Yet nature does not always run smoothly.

As late as it is, a young cow is ready to breed. At noon she moves from the middle of the herd to the outside, where the bulls stand.

Henry Rush snaps another picture and misses getting the flip. He caterpillars closer. Red Dog sees him and whistles, flips, and dives. His townsmen vanish underground. Not a prairie dog can be seen.

As Henry adjusts his camera, he hears the boss buffalo bellow. The herd stands chest deep in windflowers and asters. The animals' massive, mammothlike heads and humped backs are silhouetted against the rolling land. They are not eating as they usually do, but are looking west.

Henry Rush looks west. A dark cloud hangs over the sweeping miles of prairie near the horizon. It breeds bolts of lightning that flash to the ground.

Red Dog comes out of his burrow and barks a greeting to his neighbor. He sits up on his cone. Henry Rush is lying quietly on his stomach. His camera is focused.

A wind devil, a small tornado of dust, starts at one end of prairie dog town, spins to the other, and vanishes.

"Spooky little things," comments Henry, and glances at the purple-blue cloud above the prairie grass.

At 2:30 P.M. the bull elk bugles and trots into the river bottomland. A young male is on his land and he is warning him to stay away.

The bull elk wears a dark-brown mane on his neck. He carries his enormous antlers tilted back, his nose up; and he measures above six feet at the shoulders. His pale rump is like a traffic signal. He flashes it toward his harem to warn them of the stranger. They dash into the woods.

He bugles once more, a reed organ-like sound:

A a aie eeeeeeeeeeee-eough e-uh, e-uh!

The young buck trots toward the emperor bull. The bull charges him, lips parted, antlers back. He is a terrible sight. The young buck runs. The fight is over. Elk rarely strike each other when doing battle.

A monarch butterfly on her way to the lava mountains of Mexico from Pennsylvania feels the air temperature rise. The warmth makes her more active, and she flies rapidly in the 90-degree heat.

Henry Rush slows down in the heat. He is hot and tired. But he does not leave his post. He is determined to get his picture.

The bull buffalo sniffs. The air smells of the arriving tornado. He would run to

27

the protection of the lowlands were it not for the bull who is second to him in the hierarchy of the herd. He is approaching the young cow who is ready to breed. This the boss bull will not tolerate.

Red Dog whistles. Henry Rush sees what is bothering the prairie dog. A round-faced burrowing owl is standing in the entrance to his burrow. Many creatures of the prairie move into the prairie dogs' homes to find safety from the burning sun, the blizzards of winter, and the floodwaters of storms. The cones'

exits are twelve or more inches above ground level, high enough to protect against even the worst prairie deluge. In the summer the burrows insulate against the withering heat, in winter against the stinging cold. Many small animals know this. Snakes crawl down into the warm labyrinths of prairie dog town, as do cottontail rabbits, mice, horned and boomer lizards, skunks, and fleas. The burrowing owls actually nest in the even temperature of the underground rooms and corridors.

Usually the prairie dogs let them stay, but at this hour Red Dog feels the electricity in the air, and he is irritable. He grinds his teeth together, sounding like a rattlesnake. The six-inch-tall owl runs on long legs out of Red Dog's burrow and into another.

The storm darkens Sacred Mountain.

Chapter 5

The bull buffalo paws the ground and rolls in the dust. He gets to his feet and snorts at his rival, then turns his attention from the battle to the storm. As he does, the rival bull charges him. The boss bull turns with a graceful pivot and slams his forehead against his rival's. Their horns click as they meet.

The bulls shove, each with one ton of weight behind him. Head to head they push. The whites of the boss bull's eyes flash.

A male tarantula sees the day darken and runs out of his den, thinking it is twilight. Tarantulas are creatures of the dusk and the night. This fellow is ten years old and ready to be a father. He is off to court a mate. Blithely he climbs Henry Rush's boot.

Red Dog whistles. Henry snaps the camera.

"Missed!"

The boss buffalo backs up, lunges, and strikes his rival a powerful blow.

Two more wind devils spin across prairie dog town.

Henry Rush sees the light fade and glances at the roiling cloud that is covering the sun.

The rival buffalo staggers backward. He turns and trots off, thereby admitting defeat. Another bull trots up to him and hits him with his head. They push and shove. Inspired by the battles of the older bulls, two younger bulls strike heads and shove. The cows and calves chew their cuds, seemingly unconcerned.

Two six-month-old bulls trot up to each other and rub heads, then stand still, not knowing what to do next. They are still learning.

At last the storm takes the boss bull's full attention. Again he focuses his brown eyes on the escape route through prairie dog town. He still does not see Henry Rush. He can see only things that are moving.

The tarantula climbs down the other side of Henry's boot. Feeling the brewing storm, he runs swiftly on all eight legs for his burrow. A wasp with bright yellow wings drops to the ground behind him. She is a tarantula wasp. Tarantulas are her prey. The tarantula runs. She runs. He turns. She turns. He lifts his poison fangs to kill her and, like an arrow, she speeds under his hairy legs and stings his abdomen.

He runs. She runs, staying right under him. She stings him again. The poison shoots through his body. He runs. She runs—always beneath him.

The poison slows him down, and finally he stops. He is paralyzed. He cannot move.

A coyote who has been hunting wild turkey by Quanah Lake smells the air, feels the electrical currents, and trots off to his den nearby. He frightens a curlew.

Chapter 6

At 4:15 P.M. Henry Rush notices Red Dog's whiskers twitching, the signal he gives before he leaps. Henry waits without moving a finger. The camera is pointed and focused. The little rodent is sitting straight up on his haunches, his paws flailing, his teeth rattling. Something terrible is about to happen, his body language and those teeth sounds say.

The wasp senses this too. She races to finish her work before the disaster. She drags the tarantula, who is twelve times bigger than she, across prairie dog town looking for a soft spot to bury him. Then she will lay an egg in him, and in spring the egg will hatch into a larva who will feed on the living but paralyzed tarantula.

The air pressure drops abruptly, warning the wasp to find shelter. She will not let go of her prize. She feels with her antennae for a place to dig.

Trotting through the meadow above Quanah Creek comes the herd of longhorns. They are loping toward the safety of the lowland, where prairie dog town lies. A red-shouldered hawk takes off

from a dead tree along the creek. A flock of redheaded ducks who are migrating southward hastily leaves Quanah Lake, calling in alarm. The great blue heron hears them, stops stalking fish, and hunches down in the reeds.

At 4:45 P.M. the light is yellow-black and ominous.

Red Dog whistles and . . . *click* . . . back flips.

"Got it," shouts Henry Rush. "Got . . .

". . . The buffalo are stampeding!" He dashes behind the tree.

The meadow by Quanah Lake is covered with billowing dust. Black heads and white horns show over the top of the swirling cloud churned up by the stampeding feet. The buffalo gallop toward Henry like a roaring avalanche. A stick cracks. That is all it takes. The stampeding buffalo turn and thunder back toward Quanah Lake.

Prairie dog town is deserted. Everyone is underground. The vast miles of grass on the prairie flatten out under a powerful wind. Birds drop to the ground. Badgers and skunks hide.

The raging cloud spins into a funnel.

"Tornado," whispers Henry Rush. "What a picture." He snaps the shutter.

"My gosh, it's coming this way!" He looks for a low spot in the land.

The buffalo turn at the stream edge. They snort in fear, panic, and trample a fallen cow. They thunder toward prairie dog town once more, bellowing as loudly as the wind that buffets their huge bodies.

As the black funnel descends, they drop to their knees and roll to the ground.

Henry Rush sees them go down and drops to the ground too.

The tip of the funnel roars ten feet above his head like a thousand speeding freight trains. Rocks spin in the air, riding the powerful wind like paper. The sound is of screaming and roaring and all things exploding. The tornado touches down at the far edge of prairie dog town and wipes out everything— grass, trees, and creatures.

Chapter 7

Henry holds his head and closes his eyes.

Rain gushes down as if released from a fire hydrant. In seconds prairie dog town is a lake. Only the cones stand above the flood, and the tunnels and bedrooms do not fill with water.

Within two minutes the terror is over. Rocks and trees and leaves fall to earth a mile away. There is silence in prairie dog town.

Presently Red Dog appears on his cone and barks, "All is well."

Henry looks up. The tornado is high in the sky, a small black funnel that looks as innocent as a teacup.

The torrential rain stops; the buffalo get to their feet. They shake the debris from their fur. A lark sings. The tarantula wasp lies miles to the east, dead beneath a fallen rock. Her egg is unlaid.

The bull elk stands calmly under a pecan tree. Not a hair on his body is ruffled. The tornado went to the south of him.

Henry Rush gets up and runs. He has had enough. He is lucky to be alive. A patch of forest on Sacred Mountain has been pulled up by the roots and dropped on a riverbank. A wide swath

of grass through the prairie has been mowed, sucked up into the wind funnel, and scattered on the mountain. Tornadoes touch down, destroy, and lift up again as they skip across the land. They can touch down many times before they lose their power and fade.

Henry reaches the sign. It has been clipped off and dumped in Quanah Lake. But the post stands firmly upright.

He waves as he sees his father's truck bumping down the road.

"Wait 'til I get home tonight and Mom asks, 'What did you do today?'" Henry says, climbing into his seat. "WOW!"

The truck drives off. The wind- and rain-beaten prairie grasses slowly rise. The killdeer walks with its family out from behind a large stone. The prairie horned larks preen quietly under their umbrellas of flowers and grass. The eagle soars again, and the water vanishes into the dry ground.

At 7:16 P.M. the sun reaches the horizon. The sky is partially cloudy. Prairie dog town is closed down for the night. Not even that excellent sentinel, Red Dog, is out.

A gust of wind picks up a seed of the devil's darning needle. It is spun through the air by its long spiral tail. The wind dies. The seed falls to earth, head down, tail up.

Another gust blows against the spiral tail and turns it like a screw, twisting the seed into the soil.

It is planted. Another year both ends and begins on the prairie.

The sun sets at 7:18 P.M., coloring the prairie grass rose-gray and lavender for as far as an eagle can see.

Bibliography

Burt, William H., and Richard P. Grossenheider. *A Field Guide to the Mammals.* Boston: Houghton Mifflin, 1976.

Chace, G. Earl. *Wonders of Prairie Dogs.* New York: Dodd, Mead Wonder Books, 1980.

Chandler, S. Robbins, Bertel Brunn, and Herbert S. Zim. *Birds of North America.* New York: Golden Press, 1966.

Costello, David. *The Prairie World, Plants and Animals of the Grassland Sea.* New York: T. Y. Crowell, 1969.

Crosby, Alexander L. *Tarantulas.* New York: Walker & Co., 1981.

Grisham, Noel. *Buffalo and Indians on the Great Plains.* New York: Eakin Press, 1985.

Lerner, Carol. *Seasons of the Tall Grass Prairie.* Children's Press, 1983.

Phillips Petroleum Company. *Pasture and Range Plants.* Bartlesville, Okla. 74004, 1963.

Rowan, James P. *Prairies and Grasslands.* Children's Press, 1983.

Scott, Jack Denton. *Little Dogs of the Prairie.* New York: Putnam, 1977.

Victor, Joan B. *Tarantulas.* New York: Dodd, Mead, 1979.

Vyn, Kathleen. *The Prairie Community.* New York: Messner, 1978.

Index

Numbers in *italics* refer to illustrations.

Don't miss this *One Day* chapter book:

One Day in the ALPINE TUNDRA

by *Jean Craighead George*
illustrated by Walter Gaffney-Kessell

Over the alpine tundra, the land above the trees on a high mountaintop, hangs an enormous rock. Below the rock, a pocket gopher tunnels underground, storing away seeds for winter. The rabbitlike pika begins her harvest of grass and wildflowers. And a boy named Johnny rolls over in his tent as he wakes up for the day.

Suddenly, the great rock slips. After centuries of cracking in the cold and the heat, the slab is now poised to fall—and change the face of the alpine tundra forever.

Published by Harper Trophy Paperback Books

Don't miss this *One Day* chapter book:

One Day in the DESERT

by Jean Craighead George
illustrated Fred Brenner

As day breaks in the Sonoran Desert of Arizona, a wounded mountain lion limps toward a Papago Indian hut. The lion fears people, but today he is desperately hungry. And he has caught the scent of Birdwing and her mother.

Then a loud thunderclap warns Birdwing, the mountain lion, and all the creatures of the desert that danger is near. A flood will soon wash over the land—and some will not survive it.

Published by Harper Trophy Paperback Books